BACKYARD
COMPOSTING

Your C
Recycli

Harmonious Technologies

 **Harmonious Press**
Ojai, California

This book printed on recycled paper

First Printing 1992
Second Printing 1992, Revised
Third Printing 1992, Revised
Fourth Printing 1992, Revised
Fifth Printing 1992, Revised
Sixth Printing 1993, Revised

Author and Publisher: John W. Roulac
Editor: Marialyce Pedersen
Cover Design: Robert Howard
Film Output: Graphic Traffic
Printing: Patterson Printing
Typesetting: J. Robin & Associates

ISBN 0-9629768-0-6
CIP 91-073105

The information contained in this book is true and complete
to the best of our knowledge. However, no guarantees are placed
on the results. The responsibilities lie with the reader.

If your local bookstore, retailer or catalog
is out of BACKYARD COMPOSTING,
Call (800) 247-6553
24 hours a day, 7 days a week
Master Card/Visa accepted.

Bulk rates available. Contact:
Harmonious Press
P.O. Box 1865-100
Ojai, CA 93024
(805) 646-8030

Acknowledgments

The following people provided invaluable technical review:

Dr. Tony Dominski, education director,
Community Environmental Council

Dr. Clark Gregory, "Compost Man,"
Atlanta, Georgia

Richard Kashmanian, senior economist,
US Environmental Protection Agency

Matthew Werner, soil ecologist,
Agroecology Program, UC Santa Cruz

Sherl Hopkins, University of California
Cooperative Extension Service, L.A. County

Ruth Richardson, master composter,
Recycling Council of Ontario

Jim McNelly, president,
McNelly Group

Dr. Bill Roley, director,
Permaculture Institute of Southern California

All philosophical conclusions are the
sole responsibility of Harmonious Technologies.

Harmonious Technologies would like to thank everyone
who provided inspiration and assistance in creating
this book, including:

Don Sexton
Carl & Nan Tolbert
Jerry Moles
Robert W. Tansill
Isabel Adams
Taryn Henry
Jeff Hunts

Howard Westley
Dan Poynter
Julia Russell
Bill Mollison
John Perlin
Brenda Burglas
Peter Dukich
Lynne Blackman

Steven Zien
George Stevens
Stephan Reeve
Hari Khalsa
Bob Walters
Bruce Braunstein
Mark Walsh

Table of Contents

Introduction

The Earth has been having a tough time lately – overflowing landfills, loss of rainforests, air pollution, chemical poisoning, soil erosion and disappearing ozone layer.

Much of this is the result of how we live. Thinking about or implementing change on a national or global basis can be overwhelming. Now you can do something for the part of the Earth you live with day by day – your backyard. Backyard composting follows basic values, such as putting things where they belong and not making a mess.

Composting at home reduces your personal volume of trash, conserves water, increases plant growth, replaces the need for harsh chemical fertilizers and pesticides and it is also fun. While you may not win an environmental hero of the year award, your trees, earthworms, butterflies and other flora and fauna will be thankful for your composting achievements.

In the following pages, you will find everything you need to know to start your adventure in composting.

Harmonious Technologies

Crash Course in Composting

Composting is like cooking, with many variations and recipes. Here is the basic approach:

All composting "ingredients" generally fall under one of two categories –"browns" or "greens". Browns are dry materials such as wood chips, dried leaves, grass and other plants. Greens are fresh moist materials such as grass cuttings and food scraps (avoid meats, fats and grease).

1. Collect as much browns and greens as you can to start your compost pile. An optimal size is about 3-4' square. Larger piles tend to hold moisture better and decompose faster.

2. Place equal amounts of browns and greens in a heap or bin. Always cover food scraps with other composting materials.

3. Soak with water to create uniform dampness (damp as a wrung-out sponge). Cover pile with tarp or other material to keep moisture in and prevent oversoaking from rain.

For quicker composting (1-3 months):
- Chop materials into smaller pieces
- Alternate 3" to 6" layers of greens and browns
- Mix the pile by turning and stirring

For slower composting (3-6 months plus):
- Just keep adding materials to the pile or bin — it's that simple!

Troubleshooting:
- Odors? Turn and add brown materials
- Dry pile? Add water, greens and mix

(see page 35 for hot composting recipes)

Composting
Questions & Answers

What is composting?

Composting is the natural process of decomposition and recycling of organic material into a humus-rich soil amendment known as compost.

Is composting considered recycling?

Yes. Composting is nature's way of recycling. The U.S. Environmental Protection Agency includes composting in its definitions of recycling.

Are yard clippings waste?

No, just as a glass bottle is a valuable resource, so are yard clippings. Glass is scrap material waiting to be melted and reformed, while leaves, grass, food scraps and paper towels are organic materials waiting to be converted into compost.

How many homes in North America are composting?

Over four million and growing daily.

What percentage of the United States' household trash is yard clippings and kitchen scraps?

Approximately 30%.

Why shouldn't organic materials go to the landfill?

In a landfill, organic matter reacts with other materials and creates toxic leachate that may contaminate

nearby streams or groundwater. Also, the majority of North American landfills will be full by the year 2000.

How does compost benefit the soil?

Compost improves soil structure, texture and aeration and increases its water-holding capacity. Compost loosens clay soils and helps sandy soils retain water. Adding compost to soils aids in erosion control, promotes soil fertility and stimulates healthy root development in plants.

When was the first recorded use of compost to enhance soil fertility in Western Civilization?

The Roman Statesman Marcus Cato introduced composting as a way to build soil fertility through-out the Roman Empire more than 2,000 years ago.

Can compost replace petroleum-based fertilizers?

Yes, generous amounts of rich compost can supply needed nutrients for healthy plant growth. In addition, planting green cover crops such as clover or vetch can significantly boost nitrogen levels in the soil.

Do I need a bin to make compost?

No. Compost can be made in open piles. However, bins help keep piles neat, retain heat and moisture and are appropriate for many urban situations.

What does ready-to-use compost look like?

Compost is dark brown or black, crumbly, humus-rich topsoil with a sweet aroma of good Earth. It is perfect for potting soil.

How long does it take to produce compost?

The composting process can take as little as one month or as long as 12 – 24 months. Factors include techniques used, seasonal temperatures, the balance of brown and green materials and moisture levels.

What role does the ratio of browns and greens play in decomposition?

By having a balance of wet, green materials (grass clippings, food scraps, manures) and dry, brown materials (dry leaves and woody materials), compost piles generate high temperatures and slowly simmer and create compost. Using only brown materials in the pile will slow down the composting process because piles do not generate sufficient heat. And, by adding only wet, green materials without dry, brown bulking agents like leaves, odors may develop.

What role does moisture content play in decomposition?

Keeping your pile moist but not soaked will provide a friendly and safe environment for microorganisms (bacteria and fungi) which assist in the process of decomposition.

Should compost piles be covered?

In hotter climates, a cover will retain a compost pile's moisture. Plastic, wood chips or straw can be used. Covering helps to keep piles moist in summer and prevents them from getting too soggy in the rain or snow.

Does the compost pile have a smell?

Fresh compost has a pleasant aroma. Foul odors only occur where there is a lack of oxygen or too much wet, green material and too little brown material. Odors can be alleviated by turning or poking the pile and mixing green and brown materials together.

What is mulch?

Mulch is any material (wood chips, paper, rocks) placed over the soil to reduce evaporation and erosion, prevent weed growth and insulate plants from extreme temperature changes.

What is the difference between compost and mulch?

Compost is a ready-to-use soil enricher that looks and feels like dark, crumbly soil. Mulch is any material used to cover soil in order to retain moisture and suppress weeds. Shredded yard clippings make an excellent mulch. Compost can also be used as a mulch.

How much time is needed to compost?

A low-maintenance composting recycler's approach will require as little as five minutes per week, which is less time than it takes to bag leaves or clippings, tie them and haul them to the curb. A composting connoisseur may spend 10 – 15 minutes a week, and will produce compost faster and of finer texture.

1   *Compost Happens*

W E CAN OBSERVE the process of composting by walking through a lush forest and scooping up a layer of fallen leaves under a huge tree. The top layers are recognizable as leaves, twigs and needles. But below these are last season's leaves, which have been transformed into rich, crumbly soil. We call this process decomposition, and it has been occurring for millions of years.

As we explore composting further, remember that compost unfailingly happens, just as the leaves from the forest floor are always changing from one form to another.

We can visit the forest ten or twenty years later and the same huge tree under which we stood has now fallen and been converted into a home for billions of microorganisms, earthworms and bugs. These little critters have done such a good job, along with the heat of the sun, water from the clouds and oxygen from the living forest, that a beautiful young seedling is now proudly growing from the rich, crumbly soil in the middle of the old tree.

Compost happens, naturally, whether it is in the forest or in your own backyard. The more we understand this dynamic process, the better off our planet and our gardens will be.

Roman Statesman Advocated Composting

Perhaps the first compost formula in recorded history was developed by Marcus Cato, a Roman scientist and farmer.

Cato believed in the use of compost as the primary soil builder. He considered compost production and use essential for maintaining healthy agricultural lands.

Cato insisted that all raw materials, such as animal manures and vegetation, be composted before being plowed into the soil.

Do you need a Ph.D. to compost?

There are hundreds of well-written journals and books on the science of modern composting. One could spend a lifetime learning the intricacies of the lives of psychrophiles, actinomycetes and bacteria.

For now, let's just realize that these friendly microorganisms naturally like to eat leaves, grass, manures, food scraps, paper towels and other organic materials. When starting a compost bin in your yard, they, along with worms and insects, are your team of volunteers. They need air, water and food materials to sustain their functions. Provide a friendly "eco home" in your compost pile and nature will do the rest. There is no need to import them – they are already there naturally.

Healthy Plant Food

We can think of compost pile microorganisms as liberators of the nutrients which make plants grow strong and healthy. The nutrients they release are so wonderful and so ideally adapted to plants' needs that they are a far better soil enricher than human-engineered fertilizers. That's why we say "compost feeds the soil." The Earth's forests, which rely on decaying matter and nitrogen-fixing plants for their soil fertility, have been producing lush and fertile plant growth for millions of years without the help of any petroleum-based fertilizers.

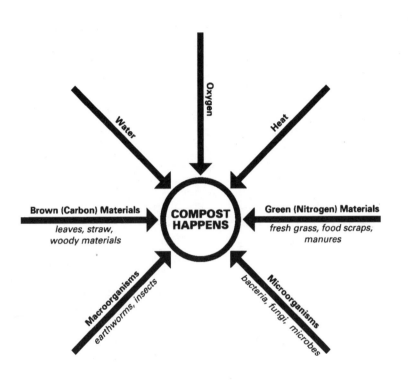

Soil needs what compost's life processes give – nutrients that release their nutrition gradually and in small doses over long periods of time.

Synthetic fertilizers provide quick jolts of nutrition to the plant roots, but in the process they stymie root development, while compost-enriched soils encourage healthy and abundant root development. Without the life process that distinguishes composted soil from soil fertilized with synthetic ingredients, the skin of our planet will quickly degenerate into an inert, barren landscape.

How Much Time Does Composting Take?

Add up the time it takes you to bag grass clippings and leaves, tie the bags, place them in trash cans and haul the cans to the curb. Now, instead of bagging your yard clippings, place the organic portion on your compost pile or in your bin – a simple enclosure is all you need.

Rather than returning every week to haul several trash cans to the curb, you only have to tend your pile in a few weeks or months. You can stir, poke or turn the pile with your shovel or pitchfork, check the moisture levels, add fresh materials and your organic materials will slowly simmer, with little more attention. Fill your bin and keep it full. The material "shrinks" as it composts.

Depending on the method you choose (see Chapter 4), your compost will be ready to use in less than a month, or as long as 12 – 24 months.

Some dedicated compost connoisseurs return every few days to add more materials to the pile and perhaps say a few compost words or prayers!

You can also use food scraps (except meat), paper towels and toilet paper tubes for composting. Store them in a bucket or food container with a tight-fitting lid and then add them to the compost pile.

If you are only composting yard clippings, you could spend as little as five minutes a week maintaining your compost pile. If you are composting kitchen scraps, figure in a few additional minutes. Remember, spending just a few minutes a week composting will transform your trash into treasure.

Mixing the Batch

The difference between a beginner and an experienced composter is quite simple. The beginner is aware of fewer pointers for making compost. The veteran intentionally takes the time to provide a friendly environment for the various elements, as shown in the "Compost Happens" diagram.

There are as many different recipes for baking a fine-tasting casserole as there are cooks. The same is true in making a batch of compost. An experienced composter may create compost a little more easily than a beginner. Yet both will make usable, soil-enriching compost. Each time you make a new batch, you can refine your skills further.

There is no way to fail with composting. It just may take a little longer, because ultimately, compost happens.

2 *Soil Fertility*

I NTERACTION BETWEEN CIVILIZATION and the Earth's natural resources has taken many forms throughout history. A conservation-based society understands that a healthy, diverse and vibrant ecosystem is beneficial for its members.

Five thousand years ago, in what is known as the Fertile Crescent, the great Mesopotamian civilization thrived in the lush Tigris/Euphrates River Valley. Considered to be the birthplace of Western Civilization, the people of this region invented the wheel and recorded, on clay tablets, the first written set of laws. They also developed and cultivated several important modern – day crops, including dates, figs, mulberries and pistachios.

According to John Perlin's classic book, *A Forest Journey*, "The ruler at that time, Gilgamesh, wished to make a name for himself by building up his city … fortunately for Gilgamesh, a great primeval forest lay before him.

"That such vast tracts of timber grew near Southern Mesopotamia might seem a flight of fancy, considering the present barren condition of the land, but before the intrusion of civilizations an almost unbroken forest flourished in the hills and mountains surrounding the Fertile Crescent … Gilgamesh's war against the forest has been repeated for generations, in every corner of the globe, in order to supply building and fuel stocks needed for each civilization's continual material growth."

*An ancient bas relief depicts
a forest scene in the Near East.*

Reproduced from A FOREST JOURNEY, The Role of Wood in the
Development of Civilization, *by John Perlin, with the permission of the
author and W.W. Norton & Company, Inc. Copyright © 1989 by John Perlin*

Later, the Roman Christian and Arab Muslim empires placed great demands on native forests, harvesting wood for ship building. Then they permitted their herds to overgraze on newly deforested lands. The great cedar forests of Lebanon were gradually stripped, as were the dense stands of the Sahara Forest in Northern Africa, which we now know as the Sahara Desert. These civilizations moved northward through Greece, Italy and Europe, laying waste the forests before them.

North America

Here in the rich land we call North America, two separate ways of treating the Earth came face to face. New settlers began "taming" the wilderness to serve them as fields for the animals and crops they wished to raise. Native Americans looked in sorrow at the lack of respect for nature the newcomers exhibited.

In the words of Lakota Chief Luther Standing Bear, "The Lakota was a true naturist – a lover of nature. He loved the Earth and all things of the Earth, the attachment growing with age. The old people came literally to love the soil and they sat or reclined on the ground with a feeling of being close to a mothering power. It was good for the skin to touch the Earth and the old people liked to remove their moccasins and walk with bare feet on the sacred Earth … it was the final abiding place of all things that lived and grew. The soil was soothing, strengthening, cleansing and healing."

Early founders of America, George Washington and Thomas Jefferson, were strong advocates of crop rotation, composting and other methods of ensuring continuing healthy soils.

Yet today, America is losing over three billion tons of topsoil a year, with as much as 700 million tons washing into the Gulf of Mexico alone. Perhaps it's time now to heed the words of President Franklin Roosevelt: "The nation that destroys its soil destroys itself."

In the Dust Bowl days of the 1930s, President Roosevelt signed legislation that helped create more than 3,000 local soil and water conservation districts whose job it is to prevent soil erosion.

The Fertility of our Future

History shows us that erosion and drought follow defor-estation, overgrazing and destructive plowing on a broad scale. It is evident that maintaining healthy trees and using compost and mulch are good for our own land-scapes as well as for farms, forests and fields.

Prince Charles, during a recent presentation at the Sixth National Conference on Organic Food Production, said, "There is no doubt that over the last few years a growing anxiety has developed among all sections of the commu-nity of the consequences of modern intensive farming methods. It is increasingly felt by members of the public that large scale soil erosion, the destruction of wildlife habitat and the excessive use of chemicals ... cannot continue unabated without ruining the countryside."

If our current cycle of deforestation and drought contin-ues unchecked, many authorities believe that much of the world's remaining forests and productive lands will disappear by the year 2000. With the soil will go the majority of the Earth's plants, animals and perhaps human beings.

Erosion is often the end result of a gradual loss
of soil fertility. Compost helps build good soil
structure, optimum fertility,
healthy root growth and erosion resistance.

Photo reproduced with permission from
Christian Agriculture Stewardship Institute

Personal Action Makes a Difference

Thinking of the problems we face can be overwhelming. Yet changes do take root when individuals take action in their own lives. In recent years, many people have started to recycle. Instead of being throwaway items, bottles and cans are now a valuable resource.

Yard clippings were also once considered trash or waste. Today, millions of North Americans are making soil in their backyards via composting. Perhaps the single most powerful thing we can do as stewards of the planet is to care for the small patches of land surrounding our homes. A vibrant, living soil, after all, forms the foundation for our life needs – food, oxygen and water. Remember, compost feeds the soil and the soil feeds us! By composting, we reap the benefits – a more beautiful yard and a reduction in water and fertilizer bills.

More than that, though, composters can take pride in having lessened society's search for more canyons to fill with trash. After all, who wants to live next to a landfill?

3 Let's Start at Home

COMPOSTERS ARE RECYCLERS and millions of recyclers are now adding composting to their recycling activities.

Personal Goals in Composting

It's a good idea to define your personal goals in composting. Are you a composting recycler whose purpose is to reduce your personal volume of stuff going to landfills, mass burn incinerators or sewer plants, with the added side benefit of returning organic matter back into the soil?

Or, are you a composting connoisseur whose major objective is to produce plenty of fabulous nutrient-rich compost for your garden?

The compost connoisseur will often concentrate more on the fine points of composting while the compost recycler will pursue a low-maintenance, timesaving approach. Throughout this book, options for both composting categories are discussed.

Composting and the Four R's

Composting **reduces** your generation of trash. After reducing in volume, you can **reuse** the compost in your yard. Then, the compost **recycles** nutrients back into soil and plant life. That's why the United States Environmental Protection Agency considers composting to be recycling. Increased plant growth helps to **restore** the health and beauty of our neighborhoods.

Kids Love Composting

Today's generation of eco-conscious kids can be a big help in making compost happen at your home. A fun and educational chore to assign young children is carrying the house bucket full of kitchen scraps outside to the compost bin. This activity brings the wonders of science and nature to life, as they see last week's leftovers soon becoming rich soil.

Landfills Are Filling Up

The great trash barge in the summer of '89 brought home the message to millions of people that we are running out of places to stash our trash. In fact, in more than 10 states, all available landfills will be closed by 1996.

The U.S. Environmental Protection Agency, many state agencies and Canadian provinces have mandated reductions in the solid wastestream of up to 50% within the coming decade. Governments across North America are now racing to comply. In Chapter 10, we will explore further how innovative communities are offering composting classes and compost bins at low cost.

Slow the Flow

By keeping materials out of the landfill, you are doing your personal part to reduce environmental problems, such as groundwater contamination and methane gas generation at landfills. Keeping food scraps out of the garbage disposal and composting them instead eases the load on sewage plants which empty into our rivers, lakes and oceans.

Choosing a Spot

In arid climates, an ideal location for a compost pile is under a tree. The shade will prevent the pile from drying out too fast and will allow it to receive adequate sunlight during the day. Partial shading will reduce the need to add moisture. In cold regions, direct sunshine is recommended. It is better to avoid placing your pile under trees which produce acids that inhibit plant growth, such as pine, eucalyptus, bay laurel, juniper, acacia, black walnut or cypress.

Easy access to your kitchen, water and enough space for temporary storage of organic materials nearby are all helpful. Do not place your pile adjoining a wooden fence or building; otherwise, the wood will rot over time. Good drainage is important – settled water will slow the simmering process down. Placing your pile on a concrete or paved surface is not encouraged, as this prevents soil microorganisms from doing their job.

Veteran composters often place their pile in a spot where they will plant the next year. This saves time and gives new plants added vigor.

Snow, Sleet or Rain

In snow country, the composting process will slow down significantly in winter due to cold temperatures. One tip is to build a larger pile and/or cover it. Greater mass will retain more heat. Like a bear, your compost pile will hibernate through the winter. If it rains cats and dogs where you live, having a cover or lid over your pile is a good idea. Too much water will retard the rate of decomposition.

Is Air or Isn't Air?

There are two separate families of microorganisms which can work and live in compost piles, distinguished by the presence or lack of oxygen. *Aerobic* microorganisms are at work in open-air, oxygen-rich composting bins or piles, and *anaerobic* ones are found in closed-air bins or piles covered by tarps, which limit oxygen flow. Both break down organic matter well.

Of course, there will always be some oxygen in closed-air piles, coming through the soil itself and when opening the bin or tarp to add materials. Compost scientists can debate for hours on the merits of aerobic or anaerobic composting, but for the backyard composter, understanding the basic concept is all you need to know. Whichever system you choose, open or closed, be assured that the right microorganisms will find your pile.

Tools of the Trade

Many composters use a long-handled pitchfork to easily build piles and to mix materials thoroughly. A tool called a compost turner or aerator may also be used to poke and aerate the pile. They are often sold through catalogs or garden centers. A compost thermometer, which has a long probe, can be used to accurately measure how hot your pile is.

Do You Need a Container?

As you learned in Chapter 1, compost happens, so a compost bin or barrel merely organizes your materials for you. Some people produce excellent compost without any container at all.

In a city setting, however, a container creates a neat and tidy structure that retains heat well, is visually pleasing and serves as a reminder for you to compost.

Please note that the listing of any particular composting product is in no way an endorsement by Harmonious Technologies. Our purpose is to give readers a sampling of product options. Any decision to purchase a product is of course up to you.

Heap Composting

Heap composting is a simple method whereby materials are piled on top of each other directly on the ground. Materials can be added immediately or stockpiled until enough are available to make a good-size heap. A small pile (2'x 2') tends to remain at a lower temperature and the heating process will be hindered. So, if you can, build a pile at least 3'x 3' and preferably, 6'x 6'. A pile about 5'– 6' tall in the middle is ideal for rapid decomposition. Once the heap is large enough, you can build another one.

Heaps do tend to sprawl and shrink to short mounds. To organize your compost, consider a simple enclosure.

5 Feet

8 Feet

Building a Bin

One easy way to build a simple, very effective compost bin is to collect four used wooden shipping pallets and tie them together. Many factories and retail outlets like home improvement centers throw away pallets after new products arrive at their stores. Stop by before the trash dumpsters are emptied and reclaim the discarded pallets for use at your home. This fits nicely into the resource ethic of the four Rs – reduce, reuse, recycle and restore. Pallets fit easily into a station wagon or car trunk.

After placing the four pallets upright to form your square bin, tie the four corners with rope, wire or chain. You can use a fifth pallet as a floor inside your bin to increase air flow. A used carpet or tarp can later be placed over the top of the pile to reduce moisture loss or keep out rain or snow. If you have a large yard and lots of material to compost, setting up a second unit is a good idea. When the first unit is filled, let it simmer and start building a second pile.

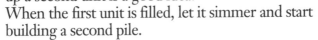

Also, consider a wire bin, which can be easily assembled from fencing. Obtain an eleven-foot length of 2"x 4"x 36" welded, medium-gage fence wire from your local hardware or building supply store. Tie the ends together to form your hoop. This bin holds just over one cubic yard when full, and is the same system that Georgia Governor Zell Miller is using.

Wood and Wire Stationary 3-Bin System

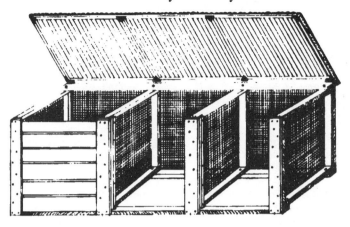

This three-bin system can handle significant quantities of materials. It also allows for staged composting by using one section for storing compostable materials, one section for active composting and one for curing or finished compost.

Note: You can use discarded wooden pallets instead of new wood to make a three-bin system.

Materials

2 18-foot treated 2x4s
4 12-foot, or 8 6-foot treated 2x4s
1 9-foot and 2 6-foot 2x2s
1 16-foot cedar 2x6
9 6-foot cedar 1x6s
22 feet of 36" wide 1/2" hardware cloth
12 1/2" carriage bolts 4" long
12 washers and 12 nuts for bolts
3 lbs. of 16d galvanized nails
1/2 lb. 8d galvanized casement nails
250 poultry wire staples or power stapler w/ 1" staples
1 12-foot and 1 8-foot sheet 4 oz. clear corrugated fiberglass
3 8-foot lengths of wiggle molding
40 gasketed aluminum nails for corrugated fiberglass roofing

2 3"zinc-plated hinges for lid
8 flat 4" corner braces with screws
4 flat 3" T-braces with screws

Tools

hand saw or circular power saw
drill with 1/2" and 1/8" bits
screwdriver
hammer
tin snips
tape measure
pencil
3/4" socket or open-ended wrench
carpenter's square
(option-power stapler with 1" long galvanized staples)
safety glasses and ear protection

Construction Details on following page

3-Bin System
Construction Details

Build Dividers: Cut two 31½"and two 36" pieces from each 12-foot 2x4. Butt end nail the four pieces into a 35"x36" square. Repeat for other three sections. Cut four 37" long sections of hardware cloth, bend back edges 1". Stretch hardware cloth across each frame, check for the squareness of the frame, and staple screen tightly into place every 4" around edge.

Set Up Dividers: Set up dividers parallel to one another 3 feet apart. Measure and mark centers for the two inside dividers. Cut four 9-foot pieces out of the two 18-foot 2x4 boards. Place two 9-foot base boards on top of dividers and measure the positions for the two inside dividers. Mark a center line for each divider on the 9-foot 2x4. With each divider line up the center lines and make the base board flush against the outer edge of the divider. Drill a ½" hole through each junction centered 1" in from the inside edge. Secure base boards with carriage bolts, but do not tighten yet. Turn the unit right side up and repeat the process for the top 9-foot board. Using the carpenter's square or measuring between opposing corners, make sure the bin is square, and tighten all bolts securely. Fasten a 9-foot-long piece of hardware cloth securely to the back side of the bin with staples every 4" around the frame.

Front Slats and Runners:
Cut four 36" long 2x6s for front slat runners. Rip-cut two of these boards to 4 ¾" wide and nail them securely to the front of the outside dividers and baseboard, making them flush on top and outside edges. Save remainder of rip-cut boards for use as back runners. Center the remaining full width boards on the front of the inside dividers flush with the top edge, and nail securely. To create back runners, cut the remaining 2x6 into a 34" long piece and then rip cut into four equal pieces, 1¼"x2". Nail back runner parallel to front runners on side of divider leaving a 1" gap for slats. Cut all the 1x6 cedar boards into slats 31¼" long.

Fiberglass Lid: Use the last 9-foot 2x4 for the back of the lid. Cut four 32½ inch 2x2s and one 9-foot 2x2. Lay out into position on ground as illustrated and check for squareness. Screw in corner braces and T-braces on bottom side of the frame. Center lid frame, brace side down on bin structure and attach with hinges. Cut wiggle board to fit the front and back 9-foot sections of the lid frame. Predrill wiggle board with ⅛" drill bit and nail with 8d casement nails. Cut fiberglass to fit flush with front and back edges. Overlay pieces at least one channel wide. Predrill fiberglass and wiggle board for each nail hole. Nail on top of every third hump with gasketed nails.

Reproduced by permission of the Seattle Engineering Department's Solid Waste Utility and the Seattle Tilth Association

Compost in a Trash Can

Perhaps you have an extra plastic trash can that you use to put leaves and grass in. To convert your trash can into a composter, just cut off the bottom with a saw or knife and then place your new unit onto the soil somewhere in your yard. Drill about 24 to 48 ¼" holes in the sides of your can to increase the air flow, or leave it as it is and have a closed-air system (see Page 26 – Is Air or Isn't Air?)

You can bury the bottom of your can a few inches below the soil surface and press the loosened soil around the sides to secure it. To increase your composter's capacity, just dig deeper – about one or two feet down. Digging also creates access for nature's helpers to enter, decompose and "shrink" your materials.

Open Air Wood Bins

Wood units are low-cost containers that utilize lumber by-products (usually second-growth cedar mill ends) and create an attractive, four-sided bin which is easy to assemble and use. The Natursoil Company offers extender kits to expand systems to two or three bins. They also offer larger units for small-scale apartment or commercial composting.

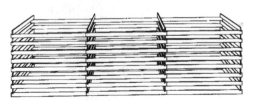

Natursoil 3-Bin

Natursoil 1-Bin

Plastic Open Air Bins

Several plastic units feature air vents along the sides and are usually constructed from recycled plastics.

Biostack

Earth Machine

Garden Gourmet

Presto Composter

Soil Saver

Stinger Composter

Plastic Closed Air Bins

Closed-air compost bins are now the best-selling models in Australia and Germany. Many people like the idea of a nice, tidy closed container. A closed bin retains moisture and heat inside its walls, and some oxygen is introduced each time the lid is opened and through the soil at the bottom. If your primary function is a composting recycler keeping materials out of the landfill, these bins are good starter units.

City Gardener

Gedye Bin

Rotating Drums

Compost tumblers are raised, drum-shaped units which rotate and create compost quickly. With an easy turn of the drum, materials are thoroughly mixed inside, and quicker breakdown occurs.

CanDo

Compost Tumbler

Kemp

Yard clippings and food scraps are placed inside a convenient door and turned every day. To assist the process and increase the number of microorganisms inside, throw in a few handfuls of finished compost, compost starter or garden soil at the start. In less than a month, finished compost is ready for your garden, and you can start a new batch. These units are ideal for senior citizen compost connoisseurs who want to produce excellent compost without a lot of physical exertion.

Solar Composter

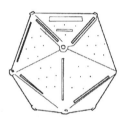

Tumblebug

The Great Disappearing Act

The first time you fill your bin with leaves or grass, you might wonder if the bin is too small. Don't worry, because nature's great disappearing act is about to begin. Remember that grass is 85% water. Return to the pile in four to seven days, and inevitably, it will have decreased in volume by 35 to 50% – and that's only the beginning. You can fill it again, and the same reduction in mass will reoccur.

Are We Ready?

In this chapter we have discussed a wide variety of home composting options. Once you have chosen a location in your yard and found a system that suits you best, you are ready for the fun part – developing the recipe and making compost.

4 Hot Recipes

COMPOSTING CAN BE VIEWED a little like cooking; a good recipe will enhance the finished product. The following recipes and ratios are suggestions for combinations you can create from the materials you have available.

Compost recyclers may opt to just "Keep the Bin Full," as described on page 44, rather than follow these recipes and mixing guidelines.

The recipes below are based on volume and listed in descending order from hottest to least hot piles. A pile made up of ¼ to ½ high-nitrogen materials (greens) will heat up rapidly and become compost faster.

COMPOST COOKBOOK

N = nitrogen	C = carbon
NN = higher nitrogen	CC = higher carbon
NNN = highest nitrogen	CCC = highest carbon

RECIPE #1

2 parts	Dry leaves	CC	Browns
2 parts	Straw or wood shavings	CCC	Browns
1 part	Manure	NNN	Greens
1 part	Grass clippings	NN	Greens
1 part	Fresh garden weeds	N	Greens
1 part	Food scraps	NN	Greens

RECIPE #2

3 parts	Dry leaves	CC	Browns
1 part	Fresh garden weeds	N	Greens
1 part	Fresh grass clippings	NN	Greens
1 part	Food scraps	NN	Greens

Recipe #3

6 parts	Dry leaves	CC	Browns
3 parts	Food scraps	NN	Greens
3 parts	Fresh grass clippings	NN	Greens

Recipe #4

3 parts	Dry leaves	CC	Browns
3 parts	Fresh grass clippings	NN	Greens

Recipe #5

3 parts	Dry grass clippings	C	Browns
3 parts	Fresh grass clippings	NN	Greens

… or your own special blend.

Spice Up Your Pile

The following condiments will add nutrients to your pile. These materials are not required, but can be beneficial to the process. Sprinkle the condiments throughout the pile.

Condiments

Garden soil * (high in microorganisms)	½ shovelful <u>maximum</u>
Finished compost * (very high in microorganisms)	½ shovelful <u>maximum</u>
Bone meal (high nitrogen source)	½ shovelful
Blood meal (high nitrogen source)	½ shovelful
Fireplace ashes (high in potash and carbon)	shovelfuls
Crushed rock dust (rich in minerals/feeds microbes)	shovelfuls
Compost starter (see next page)	per directions

* Too much soil will slow the process down.

The Lime Question

There is a controversy about using lime in compost. For the composting recycler who wants a quick fix to a potential odor problem, a very light sprinkling may help. Many veteran composters feel that lime is not necessary.

Compost Starter

When beginning a compost pile, you can add materials which will increase the rate of decomposition. If you are just starting out, try lightly sprinkling either rich garden soil or finished compost onto the pile. Too much soil will slow the composting process down. Soil is also useful if you are using a drum-type system which is not in contact with the ground.

There are hundreds of compost starters, activators and innoculants on the market which claim to accelerate the composting process. They may contain enzymes or bacteria which break down fibrous materials and/or contain high nitrogen sources. Many people report positive results from using these products. However, they are not required. Millions of composters all over the world make fabulous compost without any packaged starters.

There is one starter or activator which has been success-fully field tested for 50 years – the Biodynamic compost starter, developed by Dr. Ehrenfried Pfeiffer, a famous soil scientist and biochemist. It contains a variety of plant materials which activate the compost process in a syner-gistic way. About 10% of all German farmers use the Biodynamic preparations for compost making. See page 84 for more on this.

Yard Clippings

Leaves, grass, weeds, herbs and flowers are all ideal for
your compost pile and will break down rapidly. When
adding wet grass clippings, it helps to mix them thoroughly in order to prevent odors generated by large
clumps. As an alternative, consider solar drying your
grass clippings on your driveway for a day or two before
placing them in the compost bin; this will change them
from a green to a brown material. In Chapter 7 we will
cover a hot new lawn care trend – "Grasscycling."

Materials like brush and tree branches with a diameter
greater than ¼" will break down very slowly. One way to
accelerate the decay process is to use a common tool such
as a knife, hatchet, machete, pruning shears or shovel to
cut and bruise thick, woody materials. This increases the
surface area and allows microorganisms to do their work.

If you generate lots of thick, woody material, one option
is to purchase a grinder or shredder. These range in price
from $250 – $1,500 +. Shredders grind up the material
into easy-to-compost sized materials. The March, 1991
issue of *Organic Gardening* magazine has an excellent
review of some of the various models.

Caution is advised in composting the following plant materials:

When adding weeds, a hot compost pile of 140°– 150°
should be maintained for several days or 120° for a
longer period to destroy the seeds. Pernicious weeds such
as Bermuda grass and oxalis may not be killed during
composting and can resprout after the compost is harvested. To avoid this, put them in a black plastic bag and
leave it in the sun for several weeks. Then chop the
plants up and place them in the bin.

Plants infected with a severe insect attack where eggs could be preserved, or where the insects themselves could survive in spite of the compost's heat, should not be added. Poisonous plants, such as oleander, hemlock and castor bean can harm soil life and should only be added in small quantities.

Ivy and succulents should be shredded or chopped up before composting, or they may regrow when the compost is used. If they do start to take root and regrow in your compost pile, pull them out, solar dry them for a few days, and then reload them onto the pile.

Fibrous plants like magnolia leaves take a long time to break down and compost better if chopped up.

Plants and trees listed below are best composted separately or added in small quantities.

Caution is advised with plants which have acids toxic to other plants and soil life, such as eucalyptus, bay laurel, walnut, juniper, acacia and cypress. Having a few of these leaves in your compost pile will not harm the quality of your finished compost, but a significant percentage will deter healthy plant growth.

Watch out for plants which may be too acidic or contain substances that interfere with the decomposition process, such as pine needles. Use no more than 10% pine needles in your compost pile. Special compost piles are often made of acidic materials, such as pine needles and leaves. This type of compost will lower the soil's pH and stimulate acid-loving plants like strawberries, camellias, azaleas and gardenias.

Manures – A Compost Connoisseur's Best Friend

For centuries, farmers have used animal manure and bedding as soil amendments. Animal manures are high in nitrogen and are perfect for getting a compost pile cooking. Cow, goat, sheep, pig, pigeon, chicken, duck, llama, rabbit and horse manure all make fine compost and can often be obtained from local sources. Avoid adding feces from meat-eating animals, including dogs and cats, due to possible disease pathogens. These pathogens are not always killed in the heat of the compost pile. Remember to keep pets out of the pile.

Kitchen Scraps

Kitchen scraps are ideal for your compost pile. Instead of throwing away pounds and pounds of vegetable and fruit matter every week, from apple cores and banana peels to onion skins and carrot tops, you can now feed what you don't need back to the Earth.

Keep a covered bucket or food container near the kitchen sink. Put in all vegetable scraps, fruit remains, breads, pastas, grains, coffee grounds and tea bags. Eggshells, unless broken into smaller pieces, will take longer to break down, as will corn cobs. It's best to leave out meat, fish and bones to avoid the potential of attracting unwanted animals. While not required, you can place bulky items such as broccoli stems into your blender or food processor. By shredding foods into smaller pieces, a faster decomposition will occur. And don't forget to add wet paper towels. Some composters store their materials in the freezer until it's time for a trip to their compost pile.

Every two or three days, take the bucket outside to your bin and dig a hole 6 – 12" below the surface. Deposit your food scraps in the hole and cover them with composting material.

Garbage Disposal Composting

A convenient product for people with electric garbage disposals is The Kitch'n Composter System. The system separates organic matter in your garbage disposal and allows water to flow through to the sewer or greywater recycling system*. The materials are shredded in the disposal and then collected and dehydrated in a holding unit. Every few days, this nutrient-rich matter is removed and placed 6" below the surface of the compost pile.

*Water conservation minded homeowners are installing greywater systems which capture bathing, laundry and kitchen water and allow them to reuse this water on their garden. Robert Kourik's informative *Greywater Use in the Landscape* is an excellent guide for further reading. Many municipalities have passed ordinances allowing greywater systems to be installed. Check with your city to find out.

Kitch'n Composter

Are You a Juicer?

If you enjoy fresh fruit or vegetable juice, the leftover pulp and rinds are a great addition to your pile or bin.

Fly Away

As a beginning composter, you may wonder if your compost bin will attract flies. Small fruit flies are often attracted to food scraps placed on the very top of a pile. Do not "dump and run" when adding food scraps. Instead, bury them 6 – 12" below the surface, or cover them with leaves, straw, composting materials or garden soil. With no easy-to-eat food for flies, they fly away.

Careful

In an urban setting, the question arises whether a compost pile will attract rats. In Toronto, where more than 100,000 home composters are participating in a city program, government staff received less than 10 calls on this concern. The reality is that in most cases, rodents are more of a perceived threat than an actual one.

In the unlikely event that your pile does attract rats, stop adding food scraps, turn the pile, and check with your hardware store for animal repellents. As a preventative measure to avoid this, leave out meat scraps, fats and cooking oils. Sprinkling cayenne pepper liberally around the compost pile should discourage rodents if they are a problem.

Some municipal sponsored composting programs discourage composting of any food scraps in a bin that animals can easily crawl into.

Want to Add More?

Paper towels and paper towel tubes, shredded paper, cardboard packaging and fireplace ashes can also be added to your compost pile. It is best to recycle all the paper you can with local recycling programs and then compost the non-recyclable and soiled papers.

A Balance Between Greens and Browns

The previous recipes listed and rated materials based on their nitrogen and carbon levels. Without getting overly technical, just remember this – no nitrogen = no heat. One-quarter to one-half green (nitrogen) materials, and one-half to three-quarters brown (carbon) materials will heat up and rapidly decompose.

Odor Away

Another concern is odor generation, which is generally caused by having mostly "greens" and too little "browns" or by having large clumps of greens inside a well-balanced green and brown pile. Your solution is to generously add brown materials such as leaves, straw, woody materials or dry grass. Thoroughly blending your batch with a pitchfork also helps. It's just like a soup that needs seasoning – throw in some "browns" and stir well. Voilà – your odor's away.

You Can Slow It, But You Can't Stop It

If you ignore every tip and suggestion in this book, your compost pile will still shrink and decompose over time. With a few basic techniques, your pile will decompose a little faster. How fast you make compost and/or the quality of it is determined by your own personal efforts. But no matter what you do, you cannot fail because compost happens.

Keep the Bin Full

The composting recycler may choose to simply add materials directly onto the pile as they are generated. For busy folks, this method works fine and compost does happen. The organic materials will greatly shrink in volume, and after six months to a year, the bottom portion of your pile will be rich, crumbly compost. So, keep filling your bin, add water and relax.

The layering, mixing and fast composting methods described in the following pages are other options for producing great compost. They require a little more time and are appropriate for the composting connoisseur.

The Layering Method

Some composting connoisseurs prefer to gather and store organic materials over a period of time (weeks or months). When enough have been gathered, the pile is then started by placing brown materials such as leaves or woody materials on the soil as a base 3" to 6" thick. The next layer should be a green source such as manure, fresh grass clippings, weeds, herbs or food scraps, to a depth of 3" to 6".

Add water with each layer, along with any condiments. Proceed with an additional layer of brown, then green materials, until the pile is a minimum of 3' tall and preferably 4' – 6' tall. This layering method is the classic compost textbook approach.

Pockets or clumps of organic matter can form when large quantities of only leaves or only grass clippings are placed on the pile. These pockets may cause some odors. A way to prevent this is to mix materials thoroughly.

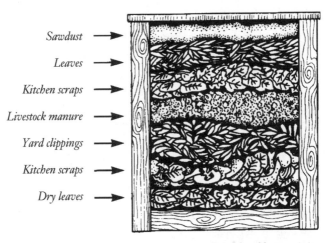

Sawdust →
Leaves →
Kitchen scraps →
Livestock manure →
Yard clippings →
Kitchen scraps →
Dry leaves →

*Reproduced by permission
from The Integral Urban House
by Farallones Institute, Sierra Club Books*

The Mixing Method

Serious composters realize that mixing materials before placing them on the pile will distribute microorganisms and balance the brown-green ratio. By piling materials on top of each other, uneven decomposition rates can occur. For the composting recycler, this is nothing to worry about. However, for a compost connoisseur whose goal is to make the best compost possible, a well-blended batch is important.

Start by layering materials outside of the pile or bin. Dig into the pile with a pitchfork and throw forkfuls of layered material into the compost bin. The goal is to blend dry with wet materials and brown with green materials. Once the pile has started to simmer, fresh materials may be added by incorporating them into the center of the composting material.

Lazy Composting

A popular and practical method is to locate your compost pile in a place where you plan to plant the next season. Cover it with a tarp or straw and let nature's helpers do their work. After 6 – 12 months, remove the cover and plant in your now nutrient-rich garden soil. Then move to the next spot and put your next compost pile to bed.

Do You Want To Compost in Less Than 30 Days?

If you need finished compost for your garden right away, or you are a Type A fast-paced person, here are a few tips from a Sri Lankan compost master, Victor Dalpadado. He began experimenting with composting systems while working as an agricultural extension agent in his country. He wanted to develop a composting business for Sri Lankans who had no daily jobs and foraged for their sustenance. His research identified five key points to follow in making quick compost:

1. Vary the materials, in order to provide a balanced food supply for microorganisms.
2. Mix all materials thoroughly instead of making layers.
3. Make many scratches and cuts in stems and leaves to provide entry for microorganisms.
4. Turn frequently for aeration.
5. Maintain ample moisture.

He suggests that proportions be about ⅔ brown (carbon) materials and ⅓ green (nitrogen) materials by volume. Breaking the skin of plant materials is very important for microorganisms to do their work. Dalpadado recommended the first turning be made on the second day after the pile is built. Turn it again on the fourth, seventh and tenth days. It should begin to cool in temperature from

140°– 160° F. to about 100°, at which point the compost is ready to use.

In Sri Lanka, groups of three people produce and sell about 15 tons of compost a month, under the name, Kasala Menik, "Gems from Garbage."

To Turn Or Not To Turn

Unless speed is your priority, frequent turning is not necessary. Many composters never turn their piles. The purpose of turning is to increase oxygen flow and blend materials. The following section discusses several ways to accomplish this. The next time someone says you must turn your pile over, just say, "What's the hurry?"

Let the Air Flow

There are several ways to increase oxygen in the pile. Old-time composters often place branches or old shipping pallets on the bottoms of their piles to increase the air flow within them. After the pile is built, an easy way to introduce air is to use a pitchfork, rod or compost turning tool and poke several deep holes into the heart of the pile. Gardening stores and catalogs often sell compost turning units which are easy to use and work well. Another method is to completely knock down the pile and then build it again, mixing contents as you do so. Every composter has his or her own individual way which works best. The fun part of composting is discovering what works for each of us.

Mats Can Aerate For You

A newly invented product, The Compost Aeration Mat, made of recycled HDPE plastic, provides passive air flow

from underneath the center of the pile. By creating a chimney effect up through the pile, organic matter decomposes more quickly and odors are reduced.

Inventor Jim McNelly, President of Natursoil, designed this mat based on composting technology developed in the 1970s by the U.S. Dept. of Agriculture. For people who don't want to turn their piles very often, this is one solution. A wooden shipping pallet under your pile will also provide good aeration.

Taking extra care at the start will pay off with better air flow and heat generation. Besides creating great compost, you can also spend less time managing your pile.

Don't Forget to Add Water

Now is a good time to turn back to page 13 and study the Compost Happens wheel. If the only things you remember are the elements of this wheel, you will have enough knowledge to compost successfully. Maintaining an adequate moisture level will create a friendly home for the microorganisms, earthworms and insects. The pile should be about as wet as a squeezed-out sponge. In a hot climate, a cover or tarp will retain moisture. If your compost pile does get dry, sprinkle water on it and the composting process will resume. In a colder climate, a cover is also helpful to deflect rain and snow. A pile that is too wet will not compost properly either.

5 *Nature's Helpers*

O NE OF THE BEAUTIFUL ASPECTS OF COMPOSTING is that nature does most of the work for you. Tiny microorganisms and visible macroorganisms will break down organic matter for you.

Go Philes!

There are three groups of bacteria – psychrophiles, mesophiles and thermophiles. These microorganisms secrete enzymes to digest the food you provide for them.

Fungi & Enzymes

These composters' helpers work together in breaking down dense materials such as cellulose and lignins inside woody matter. Three things – food (organic matter), air and water are all that are needed to keep microorganisms alive and working in your garden 24 hours a day.

Earth Recyclers

Earthworms are great at recycling decomposing organic matter into rich humus. They generate nutrient-rich worm castings which improve soil fertility and structure.

"Earthworms increase the amount of humus (decomposed organic matter) in the soil and they are important for turning nutrients into a form available for plants," according to Matthew Werner of the University of California at Santa Cruz's Agroecology Program. Many gardening and farming practices, such as frequent tilling of soil and the use of chemical fertilizers or pesticides harm earthworms and their habitat.

Either It's Earthworm Food Or It's Not

Before adding any materials to your garden, it's important to consider their effects on earthworm populations.

Researchers at the University of Kentucky discovered that a single application of common pesticides – benomyl, ethoprop, carbonyl or bendiocarb – at recommended label rates, killed 60 – 99% of earthworms.

Lawn and garden products often contain substances which are toxic to earthworms. If it's a synthetic, oil-derived product, it's not earthworm food. Compost, mulch, seaweed, crushed rock fertilizer and green sand all feed the soil and earthworms.

The next time you consider buying a product to apply in your garden, ask yourself or the retailer, "Is this earthworm food or not?" If you don't, the Earth's greatest recyclers will leave your garden.

Buying Earthworms For Your Gardens

By following the suggestions in this chapter, earthworms will generally find your garden. If this doesn't happen, one option is to purchase earthworms from a garden center or mail order company.

Red worms are a productive and thus popular strain to introduce to your garden. When you receive them, make sure they have lots of organic material to eat, preferably in a cool, shaded area of your yard. The edge of a compost pile is fine, but not in the middle – it's too hot!

FOOD WEB OF THE COMPOST PILE

ENERGY FLOWS IN THE DIRECTION OF THE ARROW. 1°= FIRST LEVEL CONSUMERS
2°= SECOND LEVEL CONSUMERS
3°= THIRD LEVEL CONSUMERS

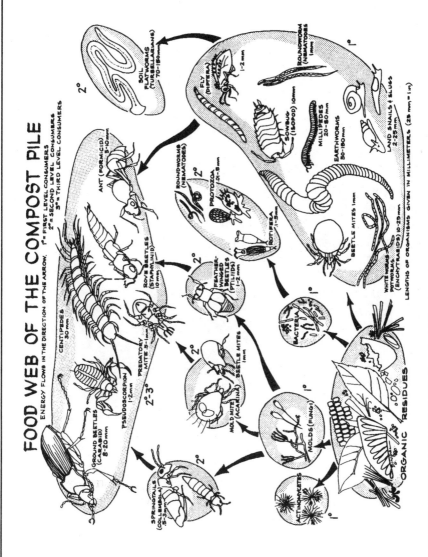

(LENGTHS OF ORGANISMS GIVEN IN MILLIMETERS. (25 mm = 1 in.)

SOIL FLATWORMS (TURBELLARIANS) 70-150mm

FLY (DIPTERA) 1-2 mm

ROUNDWORM (NEMATODES) 1mm

SOWBUG (ISOPOD) 10mm

MILLIPEDES 20-80 mm

EARTHWORMS 50-180 mm

LAND SNAILS & SLUGS 2-25 mm

WHITEWORMS POTWORMS (ENCHYTRAEIDS) 10-25mm

BEETLE MITES 1mm

ROUNDWORMS (NEMATODES)

PROTOZOA .01-.5mm

ROTIFERA .1-.5mm

ANT (FORMICID) 5-10mm

CENTIPEDES 30 mm

ROVE BEETLES (STAPHYLINID) 10mm

PSEUDOSCORPION 1-2mm

PREDATORY MITE .5-1mm

FEATHER-WINGED BEETLES (PTILIIDS) 1-2 mm

GROUND BEETLES (CARABID) 8-20mm

MOLD MITE (ACARINA)

BEETLE MITES 1mm

SPRINGTAILS (COLLEMBOLA) .5-3mm

BACTERIA

MOLDS (FUNGI)

ACTINOMYCETES

ORGANIC RESIDUES

Reproduced with permission from The Ecology of Compost by Professor Daniel Dindal, 1972

Last But Not Least

Let's not forget about the many other macroorganisms which play an important role in your compost pile. These are the larger critters you can actually see. Insects, mites and nematodes are busy chewing and digesting materials in the compost pile. Go team!

Worm Bins

Another way to maximize the natural benefits of earth-worms is to build or purchase a worm bin. *Worms Eat My Garbage* by Mary Appelhof is an easy-to-read book covering the best types of worm bins to use and informa-tion on worms. Included are plans to build your own worm bin.

A ready-made worm bin system called "Worm-A-Way," designed by Mary Appelhof, is available from Flower Press in Kalamazoo, MI and We Recycle Corp. of Milton, Ontario, Canada. It includes a copy of the book, *Worms Eat My Garbage*. If you are an apart-ment or condo-minium dweller and  do not have room for a compost bin, you may still want to recycle food scraps. An indoor worm bin will produce a fabulous natural fertilizer (earthworm castings) which indoor and outdoor plants absolutely love.

6   *Down to Earth*

COMPOSTERS REALIZE that applying rich compost generously on gardens or landscapes is a prudent investment.

A Soil Bank Account

Adding compost to your landscape is like setting up a savings account in a bank. The interest you draw from your compost soil bank is healthier plants, reduced water and fertilizer bills, a reduction in pest problems and an inner satisfaction from thoughtful Earth stewardship.

How Composting Can Benefit Your Soil

- Compost increases organic matter in soils.

- Compost builds sound root structure.

- Compost makes clay soils airy so they drain.

- Compost gives sandy soils body to hold moisture.

- Compost attracts and feeds earthworms.

- Compost balances pH (acidity/alkalinity) of soil.

- Compost reduces water demands of plants and trees.

- Compost helps control soil erosion.

- Compost reduces plant stress from drought and freezes.

- Compost can extend the growing season.

- Compost improves vitamin and mineral content in food grown in compost-rich soils.

- Compost generously applied replaces reliance upon petrochemical fertilizers.

There are many environmental side effects from the use of petrochemical fertilizers. Their production generates and releases hazardous waste and pollution into the Earth's atmosphere, contaminates our water supplies with poisonous nitrates and perpetuates resource depletion.

Harvesting Your Compost

Your compost is ready when the materials you placed in your pile have been transformed and blended into a crumbly, humus-rich soil. The heat of the compost pile will have dissipated and the ready-to-use compost should feel like good garden soil with a sweet, clean aroma. Some composters place the finished compost into two or three inch high piles for a few days, to allow any sow bugs, earwigs, etc. a chance to migrate back to the unfinished compost pile and continue their work.

Another idea is to start a new pile in late Fall and cover your first pile with a sheet of plastic, straw or other material. This allows the compost to season until early Spring when you're ready to use it.

Once your compost is finished, you may wish to sift it to further refine your working medium. This assists the growing process of root vegetables, but it is not required. Build your own compost screen from 30" pieces of 2x4 lumber and ⅜" hardware cloth.

Reproduced by permission from The Integral Urban House *by Farallones Institute, Sierra Club Books*

Clay   Clay with Compost

Compost helps to loosen heavy clay soil (above) by opening pore spaces that allow air and water to penetrate into the soil. The fine particles in sandy soil (below) are united into larger ones that can hold greater amounts of water.

Sandy   Sandy with Compost

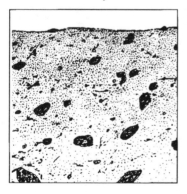

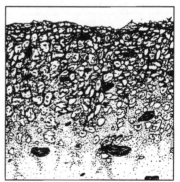

Reprinted from The Rodale Guide to Composting, © 1979 by Rodale Press, by Jerry Minnich, Marjorie Hunt and the editors of Organic Gardening Magazine. Permission granted by Rodale Press, Inc., Emmaus, PA 18098.

Lawns

To build a lawn that stays green all summer with low water demand, use compost generously. In building a new lawn, work in large amounts of compost to a depth of at least six inches before planting seed or laying sod. Another method is to use a spike-toothed aerator and apply compost into the holes made by the aerator.

Otherwise, you can sift it very finely through a screen and simply sprinkle a layer on top. In the next chapter, we will discuss the benefits of using a mulching mower and leaving grass clippings on your lawn.

Trees

Applying compost in a wide ring directly below the dripline of a tree feeds the root system. When planting tree seedlings, blend some compost with existing soil as a soil enrichment.

Applying a mulch or semi-finished compost material around the base of plants and trees reduces water requirements and protects them from freezing and drought.

Garden Beds

Add a top dressing of compost to plants, shrubs, flowers or vegetable gardens. Applying compost once or twice a year will ensure a beautiful garden and earthworms will love it. The more applications of it, the better. You can either leave the compost on the soil surface as a mulch or work it into the soil.

Good Compost Grows Good Food

Once you have produced a batch of rich compost, you may wish to plan a small food-producing garden bed. There is never a better time to start your planting than

before the upcoming spring or fall growing seasons. A wide variety of books on gardening is available at your local library or bookstores. Harmonious Technologies recommends Tanya Denckla's *Gardening at a Glance: The Organic Gardener's Handbook on Vegetables, Fruits, Nuts and Herbs*, John Jeavon's *Growing More Vegetables* or *Bill Mollison's Permaculture: A Practical Guide for a Sustainable Future*. Another good resource for organic non-toxic methods is Andy Lopez's *Healing the Planet in Your Spare Time*.

Tea Time

For years, gardeners and farmers have made their own brew of liquid fertilizer by placing finished compost or manure in a gunny sack immersed in a barrel of rain-water. Nutrient-rich compost tea is ready in three days and can be poured onto plants to quickly feed them and stimulate their growth.

Researchers at the University of Bonn, Germany, have determined that compost tea can reduce mold and mildew growth on such plants as grapes, cucumbers, beans and strawberries. Compost tea will also make a great compost starter in a new pile, accelerating the decomposition process.

Another brew you can make is weed tea. Collect fresh-cut weeds (preferably before going to seed), combine them with water in a five-gallon container and let it sit for 7 – 14 days. This liquid fertilizer can be blended with four parts water. Then sprinkle this tea as a fertilizer over your plants to increase their health and vitality.

Seaweeds

Seaweeds have been applied as soil enriching amend-ments throughout history. In 1681, a royal decree was

issued in France regulating the type, location and use of seaweeds (in that case, kelp).

Seaweeds contain rich quantities of minerals and valuable micronutrients like algins, which field tests show can increase plant yields and germination rates. Seaweed can be applied either as a soil amendment or sprayed as foliar feed directly onto leaves and flowers.

Rock Dust

Crushed basalt, granite and other rocks ground into a fine powder have the ability to "mineralize" the Earth. In Europe, there are dozens of fertilizer companies that crush and sell rock dust as a soil amendment. In America, more people are becoming aware of the benefits of adding rock dust to gardens and demineralized soils.

In Europe, experiments with rock dust indicate that it can greatly improve the health of trees damaged by acid rain. The largest study of forest remineralization to date is now underway in the Appalachian Mountains, where many trees are weak or dying. Volunteers planted 5,000 seedlings fertilized with a megadose of micronutrients in the form of rock dust, and the results are very positive.

Lawn and garden centers are just beginning to sell rock dust fertilizer. An informative video produced by People for a Future discusses current global weather changes and the important role of planting trees and applying crushed rock dust fertilizer on a global basis.

Adding rock dust to your compost piles or mixing it in with finished compost provides valuable minerals for microorganisms to feed on and convert into usable plant food over time.

Growing Our Own Fertilizer

Organic gardeners and farmers have relied for centuries on planting green cover crops which convert atmospheric nitrogen into soil nitrogen fertilizer. By growing crops like clover, vetch or beans, and then plowing them into the soil, nitrogen levels and organic matter in the soil are boosted. The plants use solar energy to do this.

Industrial fertilizer factories use energy from petroleum to produce fertilizer.

Health Begins in the Soil

Over the last 50 years, a major change in agriculture due to reliance on increasing amounts of petrochemical inputs on our farms has occurred. Back about 50 years ago, farmers produced food which was very nutritious and life-building.

No one needed to take vitamins or minerals in plastic bottles, because gardeners and farmers applied nutrient-rich compost to the soil which created healthy plant growth, and thus, healthy, vitamin and mineral rich foods.

Selenium, an important cancer-preventing mineral, was always found in fresh produce like corn. Today, it is disappearing from food grown in depleted soils where oil-based fertilizers have replaced compost and green cover crops.

"In my humble opinion, the farm problem is the greatest crisis facing America. It is basic and fundamental, and it should have our number one priority, for our health's sake. The farmers are our doctors. The soil nurtures us. Between the farmers and the soil, we have the combination that gives us our well-being for the future," said

Bernard Jensen, Ph.D., in his book, *Vibrant Health From Your Kitchen.*

Consumers of organic foods are realizing the benefits of eating high-quality, great tasting foods.

Old Seeds Sprout Again

Many people believe that seeds in packets are not very different from one company to another. Today there is exciting news in the propagation of seeds. During the last 50 years, seed production has taken place in soils dependent exclusively upon petrochemical fertilizers, causing progressively inferior gene stamina.

Additionally, old heirloom varieties were cast aside in place of so-called "new and improved," genetically altered, hybrid seeds. Since 1900, the U.S. has lost more than 95% of fruit and vegetable varieties! Yet, heirloom and native seed varieties have many beneficial traits, such as higher nutritive quality, superior flavor and color and superior resistance to drought and disease.

Alarmed gardeners and seedmen have formed a growing network of individual seed collectors and seed companies dedicated to preserving and restoring the genetic diversity of our seed stock. By saving, planting and growing unusual and old varieties of seeds, you increase the diversity of your garden and produce an exciting multi-colored array of delicious foods.

The point to remember is – good soil coupled with good seeds produces wholesome food. As a society, we will be healthier by improving the nutritional quality of our food through the increased use of compost and the cultivation of nature's multitude of seed varieties.

7   The Green, Green Grass of Home

F OR YEARS, people have been mowing, bagging, and ultimately, sending grass clippings to the landfill. Grass clippings are fine materials to place in your compost pile. Another option to consider is Grasscycling. Lawn care specialists, such as The Professional Lawn Care Association of America (PLCAA) recommend Grasscycling, which is the natural recycling of grass clippings by leaving them on the lawn after mowing. Manufacturers of lawn mowers now offer models called mulching mowers which finely cut up the grass blades and return them to the lawn.

Much of the following information was generously provided by *The Chemical Free Lawn: The Newest Varieties and Techniques to Grow Lush, Hardy Grass*, a book by Warren Schultz, Biological Urban Gardening Services, and the *Mulching and Backyard Composting Guide*, by the McNelly Group and PLCAA.

The Irony of the Grass Grower

"In my business, I have thousands of 'farmers' who grow a crop for me. This is a special crop that generates no revenue for the farmer, feeds no animals or people, but they fertilize and water it just the same. These farmers harvest the crop weekly and purchase expensive plastic bags to contain the harvest. Then they PAY either the government or a private trucker to collect the containers and bring them to me where they pay again to have me dispose of the packages and do something to make their crop disappear! What I do with it is turn it into a soil enhancer, screen it, put it into even more expensive plastic bags, and sell it back to these same farmers so they

can produce more of the crop that they are so willing to pay to get rid of. What a country!"

This storyteller, Jim McNelly, is talking about the process whereby grass clippings are bagged, collected and converted into compost in a municipal composting operation and then sold back to homeowners as organic soil enrichers.

Grasscycling Improves Lawn Quality

Grass clippings are a good source of free fertilizer and an important part of a low-maintenance fertilizer schedule. They can provide up to one-half of the nitrogen needed by a lawn. Rake them up and you're robbing your turf of food, which you will have to replace.

Golf courses Grasscycle because of the time savings and health benefits for their well-manicured turf.

Clippings Do Not Cause Thatch

In the 1960s, it was commonly believed that grass clippings were a major component of thatch, and that removing clippings would dramatically slow thatch development. In 1969, researchers at the University of Rhode Island published a detailed study of thatch, which showed that thatch was composed of grass roots.

A separate study at the University of Connecticut Agricultural Experiment Station also dispelled the fear that leaving the clippings would lead to thatch buildup. By tracing the grass clippings with isotopes, researchers found that clippings begin to decompose almost immediately. Within a week after cutting, the nitrogen from the clippings began to show up in new growth of grass.

Implementing an organic lawn care program is an important component of Grasscycling. Rapid breakdown of clippings is dependent on a live and active soil system. Chemical fertilizers reduce the population of decomposers – earthworms, bacteria, fungi and other microorganisms.

Don't Bag It In Texas

In the summer of 1989, in Fort Worth, Texas, an innovative lawn care program began. Nearly 200 volunteers signed up for the "Don't Bag It Lawn Care Plan," designed to end the bagging of grass clippings through the use of mulching lawn mowers.

Nearly all of the participants stayed with the program. The homeowners rated their lawns at 2.4 on a scale of 1 to 4 (four being excellent) prior to the program. After starting the program, they rated their lawns at 3.4 – a 30% improvement. Ninety-two percent expressed satisfaction with their lawns and many noted that their lawns looked better than they had in years.

Grasscycling Saves Time and Work

This same Texas program found that homeowners who chose Grasscycling mowed 5.4 times per month, versus 4.1 times when they bagged clippings. But after six months of recycling clippings, these homeowners saved an average of seven hours of yard work because of reduced bagging time.

Grasscycling Precautions

Proper mowing is essential for Grasscycling to work successfully. Lawns must be mowed more frequently, and varying the mowing pattern is helpful. Grass must be cut when it is dry, and at the proper height, without removing more than 33% of the leaf blade at one time. The only time to routinely remove clippings is when converting from a chemical system, especially if you already have a thatch problem. You can also rake up clippings after the first mowing in the Spring to help the grass green up, and also after the last Fall mowing to reduce the chance of disease. Finally, remove clippings whenever you cut off more than one-half of the top growth.

Reel Cutters vs. Gas Guzzlers

Remember the old days when people used bulky, hand-pushed lawn mowers? Today, there is a new generation of easy-to-use, lightweight push mowers, as shown at right, called reel mowers. They have no engines that cause air or noise pollution.

Reel Cutters Have Low Maintenance

No engine also means no gasoline, oil or spark plugs. With reel mowers, all you need to do is sharpen the blades every other season. Gas-powered rotary blades need to be sharpened more frequently, and a sharp blade is important for Grasscycling.

Real Demand for Reel Mowers

The largest manufacturer of reel mowers, American Lawn Mower Company/Great States Corporation, has seen demand increase 80% in the last three years. Over 100,000 units were sold in 1992. An English advertisement from the 1830s called reel mowers "an amusing, useful, and healthy exerciser for the country gentleman."

When in Drought

Here's a rundown of common grasses and their drought tolerance.

DROUGHT TOLERANT

BERMUDA GRASS
ZOYSIAGRASS
BUFFALOGRASS

WHEAT GRASS
TAIL FESCUE
FINE FESCUE

MODERATELY TOLERANT

KENTUCKY BLUEGRASS
CANADA BLUEGRASS
PERENNIAL RYEGRASS

ST. AUGUSTINE GRASS
BAHIA GRASS

DOUGHT SUSCEPTIBLE

CREEPING BENTGRASS
ANNUAL BLUEGRASS
VELVET BENTGRASS
CENTIPEDEGRASS

ROUGH BLUEGRASS
ANNUAL RYEGRASS
COLONIAL BENTGRASS

California Gold

If you live in an arid or semi-arid region, you might be questioning the need to have a lawn that requires importing vast quantities of water from wetter bioregions far away. In Los Angeles, at a model ecological demonstration home called Eco-Home, founder Julia Russell proudly grows her California Gold lawn. During the winter and spring, the western wheat grass and fescue grows bright and green, quenched only by infrequent rains. In summer, it dies back. The lawn retains its California Gold look until the next rainfall.

8 Just Say No

I T'S HARD TO BELIEVE that our home gardens and lawns receive the heaviest application of pesticides of any productive land in the United States. But according to a 1980 report by the prestigious National Academy of Sciences, it is true.

Toxic Pesticides

People are becoming increasingly concerned about the indiscriminate use of pesticides. "It's awfully tough for the home gardener to use chemicals safely," says Eliot Roberts, Director of the Lawn Institute, a seedsmens association. "It's just asking too much. People are using pesticides and they don't know what they are doing. The result is damage to their properties and their neighbors' properties, pollution of soils and contamination of water. It's a very sorry situation."

The most commonly used herbicide in lawns is 2, 4 -D. This chemical is far from safe. It is a component of the defoliant Agent Orange and contains traces of highly toxic dioxins.

Our government is finally acknowledging that the widespread use of pesticides on our farmland is no longer the solution. "The insects are already winning," said David R. Mackenzie, who oversees much of the U.S. Department of Agriculture's scientific research, in a *Los Angeles Times* article on June 27, 1991. "The use of pesticides is up but so is the amount of crop loss. We're losing more now than we ever have …We've pushed the traditional system to its limit, and that's where we are having our problems."

Moving Away from Synthetic Chemicals

The tide has begun to turn against chemical lawn treatment. At university and research laboratories, scientists are paying attention to low maintenance, non-chemical techniques. Breeders are introducing new grass varieties that resist both disease and insects.

Organic Fertilizers vs. Synthetic

Legally there is no clear definition for organic fertilizers. Some chemical fertilizer companies, in an attempt to cash in on the public's interest in organic fertilizers, are simply changing the label of their chemical fertilizers. If a fertilizer contains any organic matter, the new label stresses the fact that it is an "Organic Base" fertilizer.

There are no rules or regulations as to the percentage of organic material that a fertilizer must contain to use the words Organic Base. Watch out for products labeled "organic" that contain urea, a petrochemical derivative. To obtain a totally organic fertilizer (containing no petroleum products) be sure to read the entire label and ask your retailer.

Organic farming methods do not use any petrochemical-based fertilizers, pesticides or herbicides. New research confirms that organic fertilizers are better for our lawns and gardens, and researchers are learning that common pesticides actually harm our soil. Whether starting from scratch or improving your old lawn, you can do it without chemicals.

"Natural, organic fertilizers are the best type to use because they are slow acting," says Eliot Roberts of the Lawn Institute. "People have to mow them so much because they use extra water and extra fertilizer, which keeps them growing fast all summer. You get a slow rate of growth by using natural, organic fertilizers."

Organic Landscape Services

"We get calls on a daily basis from people all over the U.S. and Canada looking for a service that uses integrated pest management (IPM) or organic methods," says Steven M. Zien, executive director of Biological Urban Gardening Services, or BUGS. BUGS is publishing a North American directory of professional lawn and landscape services that offer IPM and organic techniques.

Nature Mulches in Forests

"Nature designed a forest as an experiment in unpredictability. We are trying to design a regulated forest."

– Chris Maser, author of *The Redesigned Forest*

The way we treat the land is a result of how we think about the land.

A mixed species stand of trees with western hemlock, western red cedar, and Douglas fir.

Reproduced by permission from The Redesigned Forest *by Chris Maser, R.E. Miles Publishing Co.*

9   Miracle Mulch

IN CHAPTER 6, WE USED THE ANALOGY that applying generous amounts of compost is like setting up a bank account. In the case of mulch, you are purchasing an insurance policy to ensure the health of your yard, protecting it from scorching heat, howling winds and pouring rains.

Mother Nature is a Mulcher

In observing nature, we see that plants and trees drop leaves around their bases. This assists their continued growth. A layer of vegetative matter protects the bare soil during the summer months by reducing the soil temperature, weed growth and evaporation loss. Mulching increases the population of soil organisms such as earthworms. Upon removing this magic mulch, soil life and plants become stressed and watering requirements are increased.

During strong winds or torrential rains, bare soil can be blown or washed away. A covering of mulch will prevent this from occurring.

To Compost or to Mulch

There are some dedicated mulchers who never even bother with composting. They like to add thin layers of organic matter to their garden and let nature slowly break it down, transforming it into rich humus. Depending on your objective, this can be a good, low-maintenance strategy.

What Do Mulchers Have to Say?

Dorothy Booher, Curtin, Oregon: "We grow everything from asparagus to strawberries, and all our crops are mulched. Mulch means less work and healthier, more pest-free plants."

Dick Wolf, Thousand Oaks, California: "Mulch makes my pocketbook sing. My water bill is a third of what it used to be."

Bryce Martin, San Gabriel, California: "I wouldn't consider growing roses without a 3 – 4" mulch. Without it, I'd be watering every day instead of twice a week."

Dick Hildreth, State Arboretum of Utah: "All our gardens are mulched. We use less water, less often. Mulches also look good, save labor, cut down on weeds."

Excerpted from Sunset Magazine, August 1988:
Mulch: 1988 Garden Hero

MULCHING MATERIALS

Straw	Feathers
Hay	Hair
Seaweed	Nut shells
Fruit	Leaves
Sawdust	Shredded newspapers
Weeds	Wood chips
Compost	Vegetable scraps

Using Mulch

Mulch can be applied 3 – 6" deep on top of your soil. Remember not to bury or dig in the mulch. Just keep it on the surface. Mulching provides ideal, moist conditions for healthy microorganism and macroorganism populations. Earthworms can do the work of a rototiller for you if you give them a chance.

For further reading, we recommend an excellent book, *The Natural Magic of Mulch – Organic Gardening, Australian Style*, by Michael Roads.

Shredded wood chips serve as mulch around strawberries at the Gildea Resource Center in Santa Barbara.

Photo: Dr. Tony Dominski

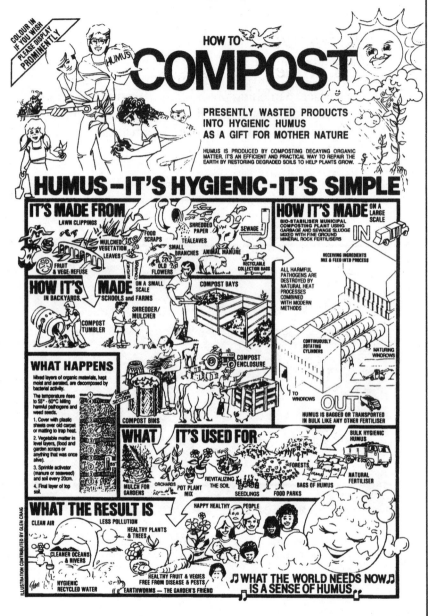

*Reproduced by permission, Earth Repair Foundation,
P.O. Box 15, Hazelbrook, NSW 2779, Australia.*

10 The '90s: Decade for Composting

DURING THE **1980s,** tens of millions of North Americans began to recycle glass, aluminum and newspapers. Municipalities assisted their residents by providing easy-to-use recycling containers for each home. These curbside recycling collection programs divert 15 – 25% of an average person's home discards.

The '90s are the decade for composting. You can divert 25 – 35% of your home's wastestream by composting yard clippings, kitchen scraps and paper towels. In this chapter, you will learn about exciting community-based composting programs around the world.

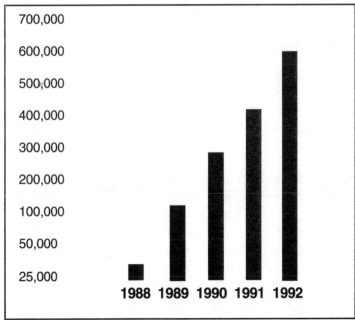

Compost bins sold in North America

Catching the Wave

As shown on the previous page, North Americans began to take home composting seriously in the 1980s by purchasing and using composting bins. As we move into the 1990s the composting wave will gain momentum.

In fact, more than 20 states have announced bans of yard clippings from landfills, and many are encouraging backyard composting of materials instead.

Riding the Crest of the Wave

Progressive and innovative communities realize that if they provide citizens with an easy-to-use composting unit and information, people will do their share to solve our looming garbage and ecological crisis.

In the last two years, more than 75,000 homes have signed up for a backyard composting program offered in the King County/Seattle metro area. More than 100,000 households (about 20%) in metro Toronto are composting in their backyards.

In the entire province of Ontario, which includes the city of Toronto, more than 750,000 composting units have been distributed.

Several hundred communities throughout North America have municipal sponsored backyard composting programs on line. These programs are easy to start and very popular with residents. As one Seattle resident said, "This program tells me that the City of Seattle really cares about me and the environment."

Help Start A Program in Your Town

Municipalities usually choose one or two types of bins, and through a newspaper ad, letter or utility bill stuffer, offer residents the opportunity to buy a composter at a reduced price. Many cities lower this price even further, giving their citizens a great bargain – a true win-win situation.

Communities save dollars by not having to haul away yard clippings to centralized composting or landfill facilities. This extends the life of limited landfills. Residents are offered composting bins which will provide them with rich compost for years, at a great price.

Municipalities can set up sites in local parks or schools where working examples of home composting containers are demonstrated and educational classes are held.

If you would like to see such a program started in your area, let your city council members, the mayor and your recycling department know. Your input will help them make the decision to start a backyard composting program. A government's purpose is to serve the people it governs, and if citizens demand helpful programs, it should respond.

For further information, contact the Seattle Tilth Association and the Recycling Council of Ontario, Canada, which have helped start programs in the Seattle area and the Province of Ontario. The Recycling Council of Ontario has produced an amusing how-to video, *The Magic of Composting.*

The authors of *Backyard Composting* have assisted over fifty cities and counties in implementing home compost-

ing programs. Write a letter to us or call to find out how to start up a program in your community.

Master Composter Program

Seattle Tilth started a Master Composter Program to train citizen volunteers in the art of composting. After completing the training program, citizens commit to spending a minimum of 40 hours in education and community outreach in their neighborhoods. A handbook and slide show are available from Seattle Tilth for communities interested in starting up a Master Composter Program.

Community Gardens

People can start community gardens in their areas. Vacant lots from city or private sources can be leased to gardeners for a few dollars per year. People can grow their own vegetables, fruits, herbs and flowers.

Naturally, these small garden plots are ideal candidates for rich, finished compost. Some gardens, such as Ocean View Farms in Los Angeles, have a centralized small-scale composting operation.

Growing food for your personal consumption is a simple and direct way to renew your connections with the Earth. Using compost as a soil enricher ensures that what you plant will be hardy and healthful to your body.

Community Tree Planting Projects

As interest in composting grows in communities, finished compost can be utilized for neighborhood tree planting projects. Compost and mulch provide accessible nutrients to growing young trees while enriching soils and reducing water demand. Tree planting projects are also a fabulous educational opportunity for young and old alike.

A great new resource for such projects is *The Simple Act of Planting a Tree*, by TreePeople's co-founders Andy and Katie Lipkis.

Degraded Landscape

Vast tracts of publicly owned lands, ranging from local roads and city parks to the nearly 200 million acres of U.S. range land (mostly Bureau of Land Management administered) are in poor condition or overgrazed, and could benefit greatly from lots of good compost. Strip-mined regions, formerly forested lands and barren hillsides left in the wake of developments are also hungry for a replenishment of good soil. As the availability of compost increases, it will become an important tool in soil regeneration. Applied liberally, it will create a permanent, vegetative cover and volunteer plants will grow and flourish.

Multi-Unit Composting

People who live in apartments or condominiums can also participate in composting. The City of Zurich, Switzerland, has 482 community composting projects at multi-unit dwellings which range from three to 200 households each.

Zurich's experience has shown that an 8' x 10' space will suffice. Wood chips are supplied to help aerate the pile, and composting chores are shared by members of the participating households. Apartment owners benefit from their tenants' composting activities through reduced trash bills. Finished compost is used for window boxes and gardens surrounding the homes. A video on Zurich's program is available from Video Active Productions of Canton, NY.

Centralized, Source-Separated Composting

While backyard composting is less costly and offers more ecological benefits than centralized composting, many communities are doing both. A central facility can handle commercial yard trimmings, grocery and restaurant food scraps and residential yard trimmings collected in specially designated "green" cans that are placed at the curb for pickup.

Centralized composting facilities form materials into long and narrow piles called windrows. Specially designed compost turning machines, as shown below, aerate and turn materials. After about one month, the volume of the piles has shrunk by 50%. Curing continues for several more months, and then finished compost is bagged or delivered by truckloads to customers.

*The Wildcat Composter mixes and turns
the compost as it moves through the pile.*

While centralized composting of residential yard trimmings is much better than landfilling, it requires higher operating costs for collection, processing and marketing in comparison to backyard composting. Home composting should be a part of all municipal composting or recycling programs.

Worm Composting

Worm composting, or vermicomposting, is much less common at large composting facilities. Worm composting relies on worms and does not generate super-high temperatures which occur in traditional, windrow composting. A major benefit of worm composting is the high concentration of worm castings in the finished compost. Worm castings are like a fine nectar for plants. Plant life thrives in casting-rich soils. Charles Darwin spent much of his life researching worms and writing about them. Darwin often said that worms are, pound for pound, the smartest creatures on Earth. Ask your nursery if they carry worm casting compost. Your plants will show their appreciation with a burst of healthy growth.

Borrowing Organic Material

From an environmental perspective, centralized composting requires more petroleum for truck trips. Organic material is being removed or borrowed from the yard for processing. By recycling – returning your yard clippings back into the soil – you continue nature's cycle of life. Remove it, and you weaken the natural system and thus, waste water, energy and soil nutrients. Let's encourage home composting and then use centralized composting, which is much better than landfilling, for the remaining portion.

Mixed MSW Composting Facilities

Another approach cities may employ is to collect garbage, and instead of landfilling it, process it in a huge, indoor, mixed municipal solid waste (MSW) facility. Giant magnets pull out the metal, and some plastics and other impurities are removed by hand. The remaining materials – yard clippings, food scraps, paper and miscellaneous other discards – are treated and placed in huge piles to decompose.

The end product is a low grade of compost. Critics are concerned about contaminants from inks, batteries, plastics, industrial chemicals and other pollutants that enter the wastestream. Mixed MSW composting was started in Europe, but so far, most plants have had difficulty in marketing the final product. Europeans are now moving toward source separation, with separate collection of compostables, to produce a clean, stable and nutrient-rich compost.

Proponents contend that mixed MSW composting is more sanitary than landfilling and the final product can be used on degraded lands or in the horticultural industry. As more landfills close, a variety of composting techniques will all help provide solutions to our trash crisis.

A composting and recycling society conserves natural resources, extends the lives of our landfills, and enhances precious air, water and topsoil, while reducing our reliance on oil.

11   *Organic Compost Matters*

N OW THAT WE HAVE LOOKED at the ecological
benefits of home composting, we can explore the
important relationship of organic decomposition to
regional and planetary health. The decomposition of
once-living materials is a subject of importance for all
who live on Earth.

New Scientist Magazine, on Feb. 12, 1987, says, "Many
of the recent outbreaks of severe erosion are clearly
linked to falling levels of organic matter in the soil ...
the more organic matter there is in the soil, the more
stable it is."

"The single most important indicator of a soil's fertility is
its organic matter content," according to R.A. Simpson,
author of *Farmland or Wasteland: A Time to Choose.*

According to the Worldwatch Institute, in 1990, the
Earth's surface lost over 480 billion tons of valuable
topsoil. Our soil is washed into rivers and oceans as a
result of the extensive use of chemical fertilizers, deforestation and poor farming practices.

Organic Farming

Organic farming is the art of raising food and crops
without the use of petrochemical pesticides, herbicides
and fertilizers. It relies on the use of compost and green
cover crops which supply the soil with nutrients.
Through crop rotation, the encouragement of biological
diversity in plants, the use of beneficial insects and
protective tree shelter belts, healthy crops are raised.

The well-recognized National Academy of Sciences published a study titled *Alternative Agriculture*. It documented the viability of organic farming, stating that the U.S. could reduce its reliance on oil and improve soil fertility and water quality. Just one example is California's largest carrot grower, Mike Yurosek and Sons. They have switched 1,800 acres to organic methods successfully. In the U.S., over 150,000 acres are now being farmed without the use of petrochemicals. Fundamental to organic, petrochemical-free farming is the building of healthy organic matter in the soil through the use of compost.

Biodynamics

The concept of Biodynamics was introduced in the 1920s in Europe by Rudolf Steiner, a respected teacher and lecturer. Steiner was approached by farmers about the future of agriculture and addressed their concerns, as they had noticed a decline in the health of their crops and livestock.

Biodynamic agriculture's aim is to produce the highest quality nutrition for man and animal. This is possible by creating an ideal humus condition, the essence of fertility in living soil. Biodynamics is a scientific way of restoring and regenerating the soil's fertility.

To learn more about organic and Biodynamic gardening, you may want to view an informative videotape titled, *"Biodynamic Gardening, a How-To Guide."*

In this one-hour video, Joe Tooker, a renowned organic farmer and educator, shows you step-by-step how to grow delicious fruits and vegetables without the use of any chemical pesticides or fertilizers. Many helpful tips

on composting, natural pest control, fertilizers, etc. are given.

Biodynamic compost preparations play a significant role in this unified approach to agriculture. They are made of certain medicinal herbs which have undergone a long process of fermentation in order to enrich them and enhance growth stimulating properties. They react like yeast and dough – i.e., they speed and direct fermentation toward the desired humus-rich compost.

Biodynamics has inspired many organic growing practices. Presently, in Australia, over one million acres have utilized biodynamic methods. In Germany, Biodynamics is well-respected, with close to 10% of farms certified Biodynamic. Alan Chadwick, founder of the West Coast's popular Biodynamic/French intensive method of gardening, was greatly influenced by Steiner.

Permaculture

Permaculture (permanent agriculture) is the conscious design and maintenance of agriculturally productive ecosystems. It is the harmonious integration of landscape and people, providing their food, energy, shelter and other needs in a sustainable way.

The philosophy behind permaculture is one of working with, rather than against, nature. In the following pictures, you can observe the important role of organic materials decomposing … and adding vitality to the whole system. Remove this process and the natural system becomes weak and lifeless. One example of this would be the conversion of a heavily forested area into a soil-eroded desert landscape.

SOILS COOPERATIVE COMMUNITY

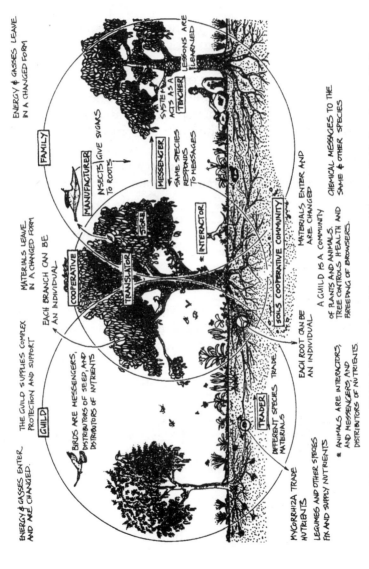

ENERGY & GASSES ENTER AND ARE CHANGED.

THE GUILD SUPPLIES COMPLEX PROTECTION AND SUPPORT

MATERIALS LEAVE IN A CHANGED FORM

ENERGY & GASSES LEAVE IN A CHANGED FORM

GUILD

Each branch can be an individual

FAMILY

SYSTEM ACTS AS A **TEACHER**

LESSONS ARE LEARNED

BIRDS ARE MESSENGERS, DISTRIBUTORS OF SEED, AND DISTRIBUTORS OF NUTRIENTS

MANUFACTURER

INSECTS GIVE SUGARS TO ROOTS

MESSENGER

SAME SPECIES RESPONDS TO MESSAGES

COOPERATIVE

TRANSLATOR

STORE

INTERACTOR

*

SOILS COOPERATIVE COMMUNITY

MATERIALS ENTER AND ARE CHANGED

A GUILD IS A COMMUNITY OF PLANTS AND ANIMALS. TREE CONTROLS HEALTH AND BREEDING OF BROWSERS.

CHEMICAL MESSAGES TO THE SAME & OTHER SPECIES

Each root can be an individual

MYCORRHIZA TRADE NUTRIENTS

LEGUMES AND OTHER SPECIES FIX AND SUPPLY NUTRIENTS

DIFFERENT SPECIES TRADE MATERIALS

TRADER

* ANIMALS ARE INTERACTORS, AND MESSENGERS, AND DISTRIBUTORS OF NUTRIENTS

Reproduced by permission of Bill Mollison, author of Permaculture: A Practical Guide for a Sustainable Future.

EVOLUTION FROM CONTEMPORARY AGRICULTURE
TO PERMACULTURE

A. CONTEMPORARY / WESTERN AGRICULTURE   **YEAR 1**

B. TRANSITIONAL AND CONSERVATION FARMING   **YEAR 4**

C. PERMACULTURE: 70% cropland devoted to forage farming   **YEAR 8**

Basic changes involve replacing animal forage grains with tree crops, increasing forest cover, adopting low to no tillage on remaining croplands, retrofitting the house for energy conservation, and producing some (if not all) fuel on the farm.

Reproduced by permission of Bill Mollison, author of
Permaculture: A Practical Guide for a Sustainable Future.

The preceding two illustrations from *Permaculture: A Practical Guide for a Sustainable Future*, by Australian Bill Mollison, beautifully demonstrate the dynamic tapestry of nature. The Permaculture Institute, co-founded by Mollison, offers hands-on workshops worldwide.

Garden of Eden

At Sprout Acres in Laguna Beach, California, Dr. Bill Roley has created a vibrant living model of permaculture principles. Household resources are composted/recycled, and food, energy and hot water are produced via harmonious interaction between nature and technology.

Dr. Roley and his family enjoy the delicious fresh fruits and vegetables growing in their ecotopia-like Garden of Eden. Beyond the benefits of lower monthly bills for food, trash and utilities, they receive a deep inner satisfaction from living in balance with nature.

Tree-Free Paper

Use of recycled paper is growing rapidly. *The Los Angeles Times* uses more than 40% recycled paper. Newsprint can only be recycled about five times before losing strength. Thus, recycling only allows us to use the same tree several times. The "short fibers," too short to recycle back into paper, can and should be composted by blending them into local composting projects.

"Tree-free paper"– paper made from crops rather than from wood pulp – is generating considerable interest worldwide. Robert Hunter, a Canadian designer of paper mills, believes wood's days are numbered. "Within 30 to 40 years, you're going to see a revival of non-woods," he predicts. "They're renewable and you get a new crop every year."

Kenaf is an annual, hibiscus plant related to okra. It is native to East Africa, and can grow 14 – 16 feet in five months. The USDA considers kenaf the most promising source of fiber for tree-free newsprint. A key advantage of kenaf is that it requires 50% less ink in the printing process due to a harder surface.

Kenaf International, Ltd., based in McAllen, Texas, is pursuing construction of a kenaf newsprint mill. *The Bakersfield Californian* newspaper has used kenaf and is very satisfied. KP Products Inc., of Albuquerque, NM is the first company to commercially produce tree-free kenaf bond paper and envelopes. The potential for kenaf to reduce our reliance on forests for paper pulp is promising. Kenaf's low lignin content makes it easier than tree pulp to process, and water from its mills can be clean enough to use for crop irrigation. Tree-pulp mills produce vast quantities of toxic, chemical-laden water.

Another tree-free crop is hemp, used for thousands of years in paper, packaging, rope, clothing and more. *The Wall Street Journal* , in the May 2, 1991 issue, published an article on hemp. *The Earth Island Journal* also published an analysis of its uses in the Fall, 1990 issue, titled, "The Forgotten History of Hemp." In fact, the U.S. government, in 1942, produced a film,"Hemp for Victory," which shows farmers growing and processing hemp for fiber, to encourage other farmers to grow it for needed war supplies. More than 200,000 acres were harvested in the '40s! Today, hemp is grown and used in France, China, Russia and Hungary.

By removing the market barriers for hemp, a wide variety of manufacturers will be able to utilize this ecological feedstock, replacing cotton, tree and petroleum-based materials.

12 *Troubleshooting*

CONCERN	POSSIBLE CAUSES	SOLUTION
ROTTEN ODOR	excess moisture (anaerobic conditions)	turn pile, add dry, porous materials, such as leaves, sawdust, wood chips, or straw
	compaction	turn pile, or make smaller
AMMONIA ODOR	too much greens (nitrogen)	add brown (carbon) material, such as leaves, wood chips, or straw
LOW PILE TEMPERATURE	pile too small	make pile bigger or insulate sides
	insufficient moisture	add water while turning pile or cover top
	poor aeration	turn pile
	lack of greens (nitrogen)	mix in green sources such as grass clippings, manure or food scraps
	cold weather	increase pile size or insulate pile with an extra layer of material, such as straw
HIGH PILE TEMPERATURE (+ 140º F)	pile too large	reduce pile size
	insufficient ventilation	turn pile
PESTS rats raccoons insects	presence of meat scraps or fatty food waste	remove meat and fatty foods from pile, or cover with a layer of soil, leaves or sawdust, or use an animal-proof compost bin or turn pile to increase temperature

Resource List

We encourage you to contact your local retailer or catalog company to purchase any of the products mentioned in *Backyard Composting*.

To receive an updated list of addresses and phone numbers of companies carrying composting products, please send $1.00 and a stamped, self-addressed business size (#10) envelope to:

Harmonious Technologies
Department PG
P.O. Box 1865-100
Ojai, CA 93024

Publications

BUGS Newsletter (Biological Urban Gardening Services)
The Voice of Ecological Urban Horticulture
P.O. Box 76
Citrus Heights, CA 95611-0076
(916) 726-5377

BUGS North American Directory of Organic & IPM Gardeners and Landscaping Services
Address same as above.

California's Composting newsletter
Harmonious Technologies
P.O. Box 1865-100
Ojai, CA 93024
(805) 646-8030

Composting to Reduce the Wastestream
Northeast Regional Agricultural Engineering Service
152 Riley-Robb Hall
Cooperative Extension
Ithaca, NY 14853

The Ecology of Compost: A Public Involvement Project,
by Daniel Dindal
NY State Council of Environmental Advisors
State University of New York
College of Environmental Science & Forestry, New York.

The Forgotten History of Hemp
Earth Island Journal & Institute
300 Broadway, Suite 28
San Francisco, CA 94133
(415) 788-3666

A Forest Journey: The Role of Wood in the Development of Civilization,
by John Perlin.
W. W. Norton & Company, Inc.
500 Fifth Avenue
New York, NY 10110

Gardening at a Glance: The Organic Gardener's Handbook on Vegetables, Fruits, Nuts & Herbs
Wooden Angel Farm
P.O. Box 869
Franklin, WV 26807

Greywater Use In The Landscape,
by Robert Kourik
Edible Publications
P.O. Box 1841
Santa Rosa, CA 95402

Healing the Planet in Your Spare Time,
  by Andrew Lopez
  The Invisible Gardener
  29169 Heather Cliff Rd. #216-408
  Malibu, CA 90265

How to Grow More Vegetables,
  by John Jeavons
  Ecology Action
  5798 Ridgewood Road
  Willits, CA 95490

Introduction to Permaculture,
  by Bill Mollison, with Reny
  Miaslay
  Tagari Publications
  P.O. Box 1
  Tyalgum, NSW, Australia 2484

Let It Rot!,
  by Stu Campbell
  Storey Communications, Inc.
  Schoolhouse Road
  RD #1 Box 105
  Pownal, VT 05261

Mulching and Backyard Composting Guide,
  by Jim McNelly
  1930 9th Avenue SE
  St. Cloud, MN 56304
  (612) 253-6255

The Natural Magic of Mulch:
Organic Gardening, Australian Style,
  by Michael Roads
  Greenhouse Publications
  122-126 Ormond Road
  Elwood, Victoria, Australia 3184

Permaculture: A Practical Guide for a Sustainable Future,
  by Bill Mollison
  Island Press
  1718 Connecticut Ave., NW 300
  Washington DC 20009

The Redesigned Forest,
  by Chris Maser
  R & E Miles
  P.O. Box 1916
  San Pedro, CA 90733
  (213) 833-8856

The Rodale Guide to Composting Farmland or Wasteland: A Time to Choose ,
  by R.A. Simpson
The Chemical-Free Lawn,
  by Warren Schultz
  Rodale Press
  33 E. Miner Street
  Keystone Building
  Emmaus, PA 18098
  (215) 967-5171

The Simple Act of Planting a Tree
  by Andy & Katie Lipkis
  TreePeople
  12601 Mulholland Drive
  Beverly Hills, CA 90210
  (818) 753-4600

Worms Eat My Garbage,
  by Mary Appelhof
  Flower Press
  10322 Shaver Road
  Kalamazoo, MI 49002
  (616) 327-0108

Weeds: Guardians of the Soil,
  by Joseph A. Cocannouer
  The Devin-Adair Co.
  23 East 26th Street
  New York, NY

Video

"California Composting"
  Calif. Integrated Waste Mgmt. Bd.
  8800 Cal Center Drive
  Sacramento, CA 95826
  (916) 255-2375

"Community Composting in Zurich"
Video Active Productions
Route 2, Box 222
Canton, NY 13617
(315) 386-8797

"The Magic of Composting"
Recycling Council of Ontario
480 Colles St. #504, Toronto,
Ontario, Canada M6G-1A5
(416) 960-1025

"Turning Your Spoils to Soil"
Connecticut DEP
Recycling Program
Home Composting Video
165 Capitol Ave.
Hartford, CT 06106
$10 per copy

"The Imminent Ice Age and How to Stop It"
Lynne Saraslan
406 ½ Laurel Ave.
Menlo Park, CA 94025
(415) 323-4034
$33.45 USA, $35.92 in CA

Related Magazines

BioCycle
  Emmaus, PA
Buzzworm
  Boulder, CO
Composting News
  Cleveland, OH
E Magazine
  Westport, CT
Organic Gardening
  Emmaus, PA
Resource Recycling
  Portland, OR

Organizations

Alameda County Home
Composting
  7977 Capwell Drive
  Oakland, CA 94621
  (510) 635-6275

American Horticultural Society
  7931 East Boulevard Drive
  Alexandria, VA 22308
  (703) 768-5700

Biodynamic Farming and
Gardening Association, Inc.
  P.O. Box 550
  Kimberton, PA 19442
  (215) 935-7797

Harmonious Technologies
  P.O. Box 1865-100
  Ojai, CA 93024
  (805) 646-8030

Permaculture Institute of Southern
California
  1027 Summit Way
  Laguna Beach, CA 92651
  (714) 494-5843

Professional Lawn Care
Association of America (PLCAA)
  1000 Johnson Ferry Road #C135
  Marietta, GA 30068
  (404) 977-5222

Recycling Council of Ontario
  489 Colles St., #504
  Toronto, Ontario
  Canada M6G 1A5
  (416) 960-1025

Seattle Tilth Association
  4649 Sunnyside Ave. N
  Seattle, WA 98103

Index

Harmonious Technologies hopes that *BACKYARD COMPOSTING, Your Complete Guide to Recycling Yard Clippings* will be useful to you in your composting activities. We welcome any comments or suggestions on how to improve our book in future editions. Please let us know how your individual or community composting efforts are going. And, if you know of a good store or catalog that might want to carry this book, drop us a line. We encourage you to pass this book along and spread the compost message!

Harmonious Technologies
P.O. Box 1865-100
Ojai, CA 93024

Order Form

If your local retailer or favorite mail-order company is out of *BACKYARD COMPOSTING: Your Guide to Recycling Yard Clippings,* you may order additional copies either by phone or by mail.

Copies of "Biodynamic Gardening: A How-To Guide," a one-hour video on how to grow delicious, organic fruits and vegetables, mentioned on page 84, are also available.

Individual Orders:
(800)247-6553
Call Toll-Free
(24-hour service, 7 days a week)
Visa/Mastercard on phone orders only
1444 U.S. Rte 42, Road 11
Mansfield, OH 44903

Bulk Orders:
Harmonious Technologies
P.O. Box 1865-100
Ojai, California 93024
Call for pricing
(805) 646-8030

Shipping:
Book Rate: $3.00 for one book;
 $1.25 for each additional book
Video: $3.50 per copy

Sales Tax:
For books shipped to Ohio addresses,
please add 6% sales tax (or 41¢ per book)

Price:
$6.95 per copy
$24.95 per video

Name:_____

Address:_____

City:_____State:_____Zip:_____

◻ BOOK   ◻ VIDEO

(Print desired quantity in box)